○ ○ ○ ○ ○

Table of Contents

○ ○ ○ ○ ○

Preface

Jo Franks

Chapter 1
A–M

ALBONDIGAS - MEATBALL SOUP

3 servings
Source: Ground Turkey Greats

*****FOR THE SALSA***

1 small ripe tomato, seeded and chopped

½ small jalapeno, minced

½ whole avocado, small chop

lemon juice, sprayed on avocado

½ whole cucumber, peeled and chopped

2 tablespoons **fat-free vinaigrette, with**

red bell peppers,

store bought

1 cup **shredded lettuce**

*****FOR THE MEATBALLS***

½ lb. **ground turkey breast, leanest**

¼ cup **graham cracker crumbs**

¼ cup **matzo meal**

1 small zucchini, washed and stemmed

¼ cup **chopped sweet onion**

1 pn garlic salt

1 " coriander

cohort"

½ cup **seltzer water, divided use**

vegetable cooking spray, or

1 teaspoon **virgin olive oil**

*****FOR THE SOUP BASE***

1 clove garlic, smashed

30 ounces **stewed tomatoes, (2 cans), Mexican spices**

½ small jalapeno, or less to taste

15 ounces **low fat chicken broth,**

low salt

¼ teaspoon **oregano, Mexican**

*****FOR THE VEGETABLES***

1 large carrot, julienne

1 large celery stalk,

see detail

1 small zucchini

*****FOR THE GARNISH***

2 tablespoons **chopped fresh cilantro**

*****OPTIONS***

white corn chips, restaurant style

3 teaspoons **low fat Monterey jack**

cheese, shredded

**For the SALSA: Make the salsa by combining all but the lettuce. Chill. Combine with lettuce closer to serving time.

**For the MEATBALLS: Crumble ground turkey breast meat in a bowl with the crackers, but do not mix yet. Process zucchini and onion using the Fine Shredding disk. Transfer to the bowl. Add pinches of garlic powder and the Coriander Cohort Blend (see pantry). Add half the seltzer to the meat mixture and combine; add more seltzer as needed to bind and fluff. Shape into 1 to 1-1/4-inch balls and brown in a large, oiled, skillet over medium high until golden and/or slightly burned for a 'grilled' flavor. Do not crowd the meatballs. TIP: two batches, and/or second pan.

**For the Soup Base: Meanwhile put canned tomatoes, garlic clove and a portion of the stemmed and seeded rough-chopped jalapeno in processor fitted with metal blade and pulse to make a chunky sauce. Add more jalapeno to taste.

SLOW COOK (4 hrs on #4 and 5): Transfer the sauce to a 4-quart slow cooker (oblong). Set dial to 5; add the broth and oregano. Heat. Transfer the meat balls to the cooker and bring to a gentle boil. Boil for about 10 minutes. Reset dial to 4; cook covered for 3 hrs, then add the vegetables. Cook for 45 to 60 minutes. TIP: For tender-crisp zucchini, add it during the last 10 minutes. Add chopped cilantro near the end of the time so that it warms.

Detail: Julienne the carrot into 1/4-inch by 1 to 1-1/2-inch sticks. Cut the celery, once, lengthwise; then diagonally slice 1/4-inch pieces. Trim the stem and tip from the washed zucchini; cut into fourths lengthwise then cube.

Pantry: canned ready to use chopped tomatoes, pre-seasoned may be used, but we preferred the flavor of the pre-cooked (stewed) tomatoes. * Keep a jar of Coriander Cohort on hand: grind equal parts of pan roasted cumin seed, coriander seed and black peppercorns.

To plate: Place the desired amount of crumbled corn chips in a large shallow bowl. Sprinkle with a little cheese. Ladle on the soup (about 1-1/2 to 1-2/3 cups broth per serving; apportion the meatballs and vegetables. Serve with salad, which may be used as a relish directly on the soup.

Variation ~ FAST COOK (60 minutes): Transfer sauce to a soup pot and heat to a gentle, steady boil. Transfer meatballs to the broth and reduce heat to a simmer (Medium, to medium low); cook meat 35 minutes. Add carrots and celery; cook 5 minutes. Add zucchini cook 4 to 5 minutes. Add cilantro and cook about 2 minutes. Serve.

DESCRIPTION: Zucchini is one of our favorites. Here they are teamed with a bright-red tomato sauce that clings to light and fluffy meatballs. Pepper-scale is mild to moderate.

AMMO MEATLOAF AND GRAVY

6 servings
Source: Ground Turkey Greats

=== MEATLOAF ===

1 tablespoon **butter**

¾ cup **minced green onions**

¾ cup **minced white onion**

½ cup **minced carrots**

½ cup **minced celery**

¼ cup **minced red bell pepper**

¼ cup **minced green bell pepper**

2 teaspoons **minced garlic**

1 teaspoon **salt**

1 teaspoon **freshly-ground black pepper**

½ teaspoon **cayenne pepper**

½ teaspoon **ground nutmeg**

½ teaspoon **ground cumin**

3 eggs, beaten

½ cup **ketchup**

½ cup **half-and-half**

1 ½ lbs. **ground turkey**

½ lb. **chicken sausage**

¾ cup **fresh bread crumbs**

=== GRAVY ===

2 tablespoons **butter**

4 shallots, minced

1 fresh thyme sprig

1 bay leaf

Freshly-ground pepper, to taste

¼ cup **minced red bell pepper**

¼ cup **minced yellow bell pepper**

½ cup **half-and-half**

2 teaspoons **minced garlic**

1 cup **beef or veal stock**

1 cup **chicken stock**

2 Roma tomatoes, peeled, seeded,

and diced

½ cup **ketchup**

Salt, to taste

For the Meatloaf: Melt butter in skillet over medium heat. Add green onions, white onion, carrots, celery, red and green peppers and garlic. Saute until soft, about 10 minutes.

Combine salt, black pepper, cayenne pepper, nutmeg, cumin and eggs in large mixing bowl. Add ketchup and half-and-half. Blend thoroughly with vegetable mixture. Add turkey, chicken sausage and bread crumbs to vegetable mixture. Mix with hands to form loaf.

Place in a greased 9- by 5-inch loaf pan. Bake at 350 degrees until cooked through and nicely browned, 45 to 60 minutes. Let rest 10 minutes before serving with Gravy.

For the Gravy: Melt 1 tablespoon butter in heavy skillet over medium heat. Add shallots, thyme, bay leaf, pepper to taste and red and yellow peppers. Saute over medium heat until tender, about 10 minutes.

Add half-and-half, 1 teaspoon pepper, garlic and beef and chicken stocks. Simmer, uncovered, over high heat until liquid is reduced by 1/4, about 10 minutes.

Add tomatoes and ketchup and bring to a simmer. Cook, covered, 20 minutes. Stir in remaining butter and season to taste with salt and pepper. Strain gravy, discarding bay leaf and thyme before serving.

This recipe yields 6 servings.

Each serving, with 1/4 cup gravy: 267 calories; 990 mg sodium; 80 mg cholesterol; 12 grams fat; 14 grams carbohydrates; 26 grams protein; 0.66 gram fiber.

BAKED RIGATONI AND MEATBALLS

4 servings
Source: Ground Turkey Greats

2 tablespoons **olive oil**

1 onion, chopped

2 garlic cloves, minced

3 cups **mushrooms, sliced**

1 sweet green pepper, chopped

1 ½ teaspoons **dried basil**

1 ½ teaspoons **granulated sugar**

1 teaspoon **dried oregano**

1 teaspoon **salt**

¾ teaspoons **pepper**

28 ounces **canned tomatoes, chopped**

2 tablespoons **tomato paste**

3 ½ cups **rigatoni pasta**

1 ⅓ cups **mozzarella, shredded**

¼ cup **parmesan, freshly grated -meatballs---**

1 egg

⅓ cup **onion, finely chopped**

¼ cup **dry bread crumbs**

2 garlic cloves, minced

3 tablespoons **parmesan, freshly grated**

1 teaspoon **dried oregano**

¾ teaspoons **salt**

½ teaspoon **pepper**

1 lb. **lean ground turkey,**

chicken or beef may

Meatballs: In bowl, beat egg lightly; mix in onion, crumbs, garlic, Parmesan, oregano, salt and pepper. Mix in turkey. Shape heaping tablespoonfuls into balls.

In large skillet, heat oil over medium-high heat; cook meatballs, in batches if necessary, for 8-10 minutes or until browned on all sides.

Transfer to paper towel-lined plate.

Add onion, garlic, mushrooms, green pepper, basil, sugar, oregano, salt, pepper and 2 tb water to skillet; cook over medium heat, stirring occasionally, for about 10 minutes or until vegetables are softened. Stir in tomatoes and tomato paste; bring to boil. Add meatballs; reduce heat and simmer for 30 minutes or until slightly thickened.

Meanwhile, in large pot of boiling salted water, cook rigatoni for about 8 minutes or until pasta is tender but firm. Drain and return to pot; add tomato sauce, stirring to coat rigatoni.

Transfer to 11x7-inch baking dish or 8-cup shallow oven casserole. Sprinkle mozzarella (use part-skim mozzarella), then Parmesan evenly over top.

Bake in 400°F 200C oven for about 20 minutes or until cheese is melted and top is golden.

BLACK BEAN TURKEY CHILI

6 servings
Source: Ground Turkey Greats

1 lb. **ground turkey**

1 cup **onion coarsely chopped**

1 red bell pepper seeded & cut into 1/4-inch cubes

2 Cloves fresh garlic minced

2 jalapeno peppers seeded and minced

1 tablespoon **chili powder**

1-½ teaspoon **ground cumin**

1-½ teaspoon **ground coriander**

½ teaspoon **dried oregano**

½ teaspoon **dried marjoram**

¼ teaspoon **red pepper flakes**

¼ teaspoon **ground cinnamon**

1 Can (16 ounces) whole tomatoes undrained & coarsely chopped

1 Can (16 ounces) black beans rinsed and well drained

¼ cup **fresh cilantro chopped**

4 tablespoons **Cheddar cheese grated**

In a 3-quart saucepan, combine turkey, onion, red pepper, garlic, jalapeno pepper, chili powder, cumin, coriander, oregano, marjoram, red pepper flakes and cinnamon. Cook mixture over medium-high heat, stirring occasionally, until turkey is no longer pink.

Stir in tomatoes and bring to a boil, reduce heat and simmer uncovered for 30 minutes.

Stir in beans and cilantro. Continue cooking for an additional 15 minutes.

Serve topped with Cheddar cheese.

CAJUN STYLE MEAT LOAF

1 servings
Source: Ground Turkey Greats

2 whole bay leaves

1 teaspoon **salt to taste**

1 teaspoon **ground red pepper**

1 teaspoon **black pepper**

½ teaspoon **white pepper**

½ teaspoon **ground cumin**

½ teaspoon **ground nutmeg**

other ingredients

4 tablespoons **margarine**

¾ cups **fine chopped onion**

½ cup **fine chopped celery**

½ cup **fine chopped green pepper**

¼ cup **fine chopped green onion**

2 teaspoons **minced garlic**

1 tablespoon **Worcestershire sauce**

½ cup **milk**

½ cup **ketchup**

2 lbs. **ground turkey**

2 egg lightly beaten

1 cup **very fine dry bread crumbs**

Mix together the bay leaves or crush them, salt, red, black and white peppers, cumin and nutmeg and set aside. In a heavy skillet, melt the margarine and saute the onion, celery, green pepper, green onion and garlic, with the Worcestershire about 6 minutes. Stir in the seasoning mix, then the milk and ketchup, and cook 2 minutes. Remove from heat and cool.

This would be a good time to remove the bay leaves if you left them whole. In an ungreased 13 x 9 inch pan, combine the liquid mixture with the ground turkey, eggs and bread crumbs, Shape into a loaf, which looks like a football, and bake, uncovered at 350°F for 25 minutes, then at 400°F for 35 minutes.

CAJUN TURKEY BURGERS WITH CAYENNE CURLY FRIES

4 servings
Source: Ground Turkey Greats

For Fries

1 (28-ounce) bag curly fries

(recommended: Ore-Ida)

1 tablespoon **olive oil**

1 tablespoon **Cajun seasoning**

½ teaspoon **cayenne pepper**

For Burgers:

1 ¼ lbs. **ground turkey**

1 cup **frozen chopped onions**

and bell peppers, thawed

¼ cup **real bacon pieces**

2 teaspoons **Cajun seasoning**

½ teaspoon **hot sauce**

½ teaspoon **salt**

½ teaspoon **ground black pepper**

4 onion buns

4 leaves butter lettuce
4 slices tomato
4 slices red onion
For Sauce:
½ cup **ranch dressing**
1 tablespoon **hot sauce**
1 scallion, finely chopped

For Curly Fries:

Directions

Preheat oven to 400°F.

In large bowl combine all ingredients and toss until fries are well coated. Transfer to a baking sheet and bake for 20 minutes or until crispy.

For Sauce:

In small bowl combine all ingredients and mix until blended. Set aside.

For Burger:

Preheat a grill pan over medium-high heat.

In a bowl mix together the ground turkey, onions and bell peppers, bacon pieces, Cajun seasoning, hot sauce, salt, and ground black pepper.

Wet hands to prevent sticking, and form 4 patties of equal size. Spray grill pan with cooking spray.

Reduce heat to medium and cook patties for 5 to 7 minutes per side or until cooked through.

For the sauce:

Place all the ingredients into a small serving bowl and stir until combined.

Place the cooked burgers on the buns and serve with lettuce, tomato, onion and ranch dressing.

CAJUN TURKEY TRIANGLES

8 servings
Source: Ground Turkey Greats

1 lb. **ground turkey**

⅓ cup **onion chopped**

¼ cup **green bell pepper chopped**

¼ cup **celery chopped**

1 Cloves garlic minced

1-½ teaspoon **Creole seasoning**

¼ teaspoon **red pepper flakes**

1 Can (8 ounces) stewed tomatoes cut up

2 Tubes (9.5 ounces each) refrigerator pastry squares

In large non-stick skillet, over medium-high heat, saute turkey, onion, bell pepper, celery and garlic 4 to 5 minutes or until turkey is no longer pink.

Add Creole seasoning, red pepper flakes and tomatoes; simmer, uncovered, 8 to 10 minutes or until most of liquid is absorbed.

Unroll pastry, separating each package into 4 squares. Place on a greased 10x15x1-inch jellyroll pan. Stretch pastry slightly to shape squares.

Place 1/3 cup filling on one corner of each square. Fold opposite corner of dough over filling to form a triangle; press edges with fork to seal. Cut 3 (1/2-inch) slits in top of each triangle to allow steam to escape.

Bake at 375°F 12 to 15 minutes or until golden brown. Remove triangles from pan and cool slightly on a wire rack. Serve warm.

CAMPING THAI TURKEY SAUSAGE

1 servings
Source: Ground Turkey Greats

1 lb. **ground turkey**

¼ lb. **green beans, minced**

8 green onions, minced

1 stalk fresh lemon grass, minced

3 tablespoons **minced fresh cilantro**

3 teaspoons **fresh serrano chilies, minced**

2 tablespoons **Asian fish sauce**

1 large egg

2 tablespoons **cornstarch**

¼ teaspoon **sugar**

2 tablespoons **olive oil**

1. At home: Mix turkey well with beans, onions, lemon grass, cilantro, chilies (lesser amount for mildest flavor), fish sauce, egg, cornstarch, and sugar. Divide into 16 equal portions and shape into 16 patties, each 1/2 inch thick.

2. Pour oil into a 10- to 12-inch nonstick frying pan over medium-high heat. When hot, add a few patties, without crowding. Cook until brown on each side and no longer pink in center (cut to test), about 7 minutes total. Remove as cooked and drain on paper towels; add more patties to pan.

3. When patties are cool, freeze in a single layer in a metal pan until hard, then seal airtight in plastic freezer bags. Transport in an insulated chest.

4. In camp: Place frozen patties in a 9- to 10-inch nonstick frying pan

over low heat, cover, and cook until warm, 3 to 5 minutes; turn at least once.

Cook up a big batch of patties at home and freeze.

Heat them in camp for a great breakfast with eggs or hash-browns (Latimer uses sweet potatoes), tangerine juice, and papaya wedges.

Prep and cook time: About 30 minutes at home, plus reheating in camp

Notes:

It's easiest to mince lemon grass in a food processor or mini-chopper. For best texture, mince the remaining ingredients with a knife.

Makes: 16 patties; 8 servings

Per patty: 73 cal., 53% (39 cal.) from fat; 5.9 g protein; 4.3 g fat (0.9 g sat.); 2.4 g carbo (0.3 g fiber); 107 mg sodium; 34 mg chol.

CHICKPEA AND CHICKEN DUMPLING SOUP

8 servings
Source: Ground Turkey Greats

=== **SOUP** ===

3 lbs. **chicken, cut in 8 pieces**

12 cups **water**

2 onions, quartered

2 green bell peppers, sliced

Salt, to taste

Freshly-ground black pepper, to taste

¼ teaspoon **turmeric**

1 clove **garlic, crushed**

=== **DUMPLINGS** ===

4 onions, quartered

2 cups **chickpea flour - (to 2 1/4 cups)**

½ lb. **ground turkey or chicken, grind special**

for gundi

1 teaspoon **salt**

1 teaspoon **freshly-ground black pepper**

¼ teaspoon **turmeric**

½ teaspoon **cardamom**

water

½ cup **cooked chickpeas**

Soup:

Bring chicken and water to boil, skimming off any foam that forms on top. Add onions, peppers, salt and pepper to taste, turmeric and garlic. Simmer, covered, until chicken is cooked through, about 45 minutes. Cool and strain, reserving chicken and about 10 cups broth. Remove and discard chicken skin and bones. Cut meat into bite-size pieces.

Dumplings:

Shred onions with grating blade in food processor. Combine onions and 2 cups chickpea flour and mix well. Add turkey, salt, pepper, turmeric and cardamom and mix well with hands. Add enough water, about 1/4 cup, to make sticky dough with consistency of meatballs. You should be able to stick your finger through it. Refrigerate 2 to 3 hours.

Dip hands in cold water and form 1 dumpling 2 inches in diameter for testing. Bring reserved chicken broth to boil. Adjust seasoning. Add test dumpling and simmer gently, 15 to 20 minutes. Let test dumpling cool, then taste for seasoning and texture. If too soft, add more chickpea flour; adjust seasoning if necessary.

Form remaining dough into dumplings 2 inches in diameter. Add dumplings and simmer gently, covered, until cooked through and floating, 15 to 20 minutes. Add chickpeas and reserved chicken pieces and simmer, covered, about 5 minutes. The dumplings may be served in soup or as an appetizer, wrapped in flatbread (taftan or lavash) and sprinkled with fresh herbs (mint, tarragon, cilantro, basil) and vinegar-pickled vegetables.

CHIPOTLE TAMALE PIE

8 servings
Source: Ground Turkey Greats

1 tablespoon **unsalted butter, at room temperature**

1 tablespoon **olive oil**

1 pound, lean ground turkey

1 medium yellow onion, chopped

1 green bell pepper, diced

2 garlic cloves, finely minced

2 teaspoons **ground cumin**

1 (15-ounce) can pinto beans,

drained and rinsed

1 (8-ounce) can diced tomatoes

2 chipotle chiles, plus 1 teaspoon adobo sauce, from can chipotle in adobo

1 cup **grated Cheddar**

½ cup **chopped fresh cilantro leaves**

1 (8.5-ounce) package cornbread

mix

1 egg

⅓ cup **milk**

Preheat oven to 400°F.

Grease an 8-inch baking dish with the butter and set it aside.

Heat the olive oil in a nonstick skillet over medium heat. Add the ground turkey, the onions, green peppers, and garlic and cook until the turkey is no longer pink and is cooked through, about 8 minutes. Drain off any excess fat and sprinkle the meat mixture with the cumin.

Add the beans, tomatoes, chiles and adobo sauce to the skillet and bring to a boil over high heat. Reduce the heat to medium and simmer until heated through and slightly thickened, about 5 minutes. Remove pan from the heat and stir in the cheese and cilantro.

Spread the turkey mixture in the prepared baking dish, pressing down on it with the back of a spoon to make an even, compact layer.

Combine the cornbread mix with milk and egg. Spread the cornbread batter over the turkey mixture and bake until the cornbread is golden-brown, 20 to 25 minutes. Let the tamale pie stand for 5 minutes before cutting into squares and serving.

COLD TURKEY LOAF

1 servings
Source: Ground Turkey Greats

5 slices white bread

½ lb. **raw turkey sausages**

1 lb. **ground lean turkey**

1 large egg, beaten to blend

5 ½ cups **nonfat milk**

2 tablespoons **chopped green onion**

1 tablespoon **finely chopped fresh sage leaves or**

1 teaspoon **dried rubbed sage**

½ teaspoon **salt**

½ teaspoon **black pepper**

½ teaspoon **white pepper**

¼ teaspoon **cayenne**

1. Tear bread into chunks and whirl in a food processor to make fine crumbs. Measure 2 cups and put in a large bowl.

2. Squeeze sausages from casings into bowl. Add ground turkey, egg, milk, onion, sage, salt, black and white pepper, and cayenne. Mix well.

3. Pat meat loaf mixture into an oiled or nonstick 5- by 9-inch loaf pan.

4. Bake in a 350° oven until meat loaf is firm to touch in center, about 1 1/2 hours.

5. Serve hot, or let cool, then cover and chill until cold, at least 3 hours. Or store, chilled, up to 2 days. Run a knife between meat and pan rim. Invert meat loaf onto a platter. Cut into thick slices.

CROCKPOT NEAPOLITAN TOSTADA

8 servings
Source: Ground Turkey Greats

¾ lbs. **ground turkey**
1 eggplant
1 cup **salsa**
1 can tomato paste
¼ cup **fresh parsley**
1 tablespoon **chili powder**
1 teaspoon **ground cumin**
1 teaspoon **dried oregano**
1 package frozen corn
4 pita bread
½ cup **yogurt**
2 cups **lettuce**
½ cup **olive**
½ cup **cheddar cheese**

Combine turkey, eggplant, salsa, tomato paste, parsley, chili powder, cumin, oregano and corn in slow cooker. Cover and cook on low 5 to 6 hours.

Stir with a fork to break up large chunks of turkey. Spoon about 3/4 cup cooked turkey mixture on each pita half. Top with yogurt, lettuce, olives and cheese, if desired.

CURRIED TURKEY MEATBALLS WITH CHUTNEY

48 servings
Source: Ground Turkey Greats

chutney sauce

1 lb. **ground turkey**

½ cup **crushed cracker crumbs**

⅓ cup **evaporated skim milk**

2 tablespoons **finely chopped green**

onions, (with tops)

1 ½ to, up to

2 teaspoons **curry powder**

¼ teaspoon **salt**

chutney sauce

½ cup **nonfat plain yogurt**

1 tablespoon **finely chopped chutney**

¼ teaspoon **curry powder**

Curried Meatballs with Chutney Sauce. Prepare Chutney Sauce. Heat oven to 400°F. Mix remaining ingredients; shape into forty-eight 1-inch meatballs. Place in rectangular pan, 13 X 9 X 2 inches, sprayed with nonstick cooking spray. Bake uncovered until light brown and no longer pink inside, 10 to 15 minutes. Serve hot with Chutney Sauce and wooden picks.

CHUTNEY SAUCE Mix all ingredients; cover and refrigerate at least 1 hour.

MICROWAVE DIRECTIONS: Prepare Chutney Sauce and meatballs as directed.

Place 24 meatballs in microwavable pie plate, 9 X 1-1/4 inches. Cover with waxed paper and microwave on high (100%) 3 minutes; rearrange meatballs.

Cover and microwave until no longer pink inside, 2 to 4 minutes longer. Let stand covered 3 minutes; drain. Repeat with remaining meatballs. Serve hot with Chutney Sauce and wooden picks.

EASY OVEN MEATBALLS

4 servings
Source: Ground Turkey Greats

Ground Turkey Greats

2 slices white bread

1 small onion

1 lb. **turkey, ground**

1 package chopped spinach, thawed

1 teaspoon **salt**

¼ teaspoon **pepper**

1 large egg

3 carrots, med. size.

¼ lb. **mushrooms**

1 jar spaghetti sauce, garden style

cooked spaghetti for 4 serv.

Preheat oven 400°F. Grease or spray 13 x 9 inch baking pan. Chop the bread until fine crumbs form (abt. 1 cup). Grate onion for 1 tbs. In large bowl, mix bread crumbs and grated onion with ground turkey, spinach, salt, pepper, and egg.

Shape turkey mixture into 16 meatballs. Place meatballs in pan and bake 25 minutes or until meatballs are lightly browned and cooked through.

Meanwhile, thinly slice carrots and cut mushrooms into 1/2" pcs. In 3 quart saucepan over high heat, heat carrots, mushrooms, pasta sauce, and 1/2 cup water to boiling. Reduce heat to low; cover and simmer 20 minutes. When meatballs are done, add to sauce; cover and simmer 10 minutes longer to blend flavors and cook vegetables until tender. Serve over spaghetti or rice.

EASY OVEN TURKEY MEATBALLS

4 servings
Source: Ground Turkey Greats

2 slices white bread

1 small onion

1 lb. **turkey, ground**

1 package chopped spinach, thawed

1 teaspoon **salt**

¼ teaspoon **pepper**

1 large egg

3 carrots, med. size.

¼ lb. **mushrooms**

1 jar spaghetti sauce, garden>

style

cooked spaghetti for 4 serv.

Preheat oven 400°F. Grease or spray 13 x 9 inch baking pan. Chop the bread until fine crumbs form (about 1 cup). Grate onion for 1 tbs. In large bowl, mix bread crumbs and grated onion with ground turkey, spinach, salt, pepper, and egg.

Shape turkey mixture into 16 meatballs. Place meatballs in pan and bake 25 minutes or until meatballs are lightly browned and cooked through.

Meanwhile, thinly slice carrots and cut mushrooms into 1/2" pcs. In 3 quart saucepan over high heat, heat carrots, mushrooms, pasta sauce, and 1/2 cup water to boiling. Reduce heat to low; cover and simmer 20 minutes. When meatballs are done, add to sauce; cover and simmer 10 minutes longer to blend flavors and cook vegetables until tender. Serve over spaghetti or rice.

EASY TURKEY SLOPPY JOES

4 servings
Source: Ground Turkey Greats

1 ½ lbs. **Ground turkey**

½ cup **Ketsup**

1 md Onion, diced

2 tablespoons **Dijon mustard**

½ teaspoon **Seasoning salt**

¼ teaspoon **Garlic powder**

Non stick spray

4 Large hamburger rolls

or rolls of your

choice, split

Either use a non-stick skillet or spray a skillet with non-stick spray. Add ground turkey and onion, and cook until meat is no longer pink.

Add other ingredients, and simmer until thickened to your choosing.

Serve as you would sloppy joes, on split rolls.

You will find this is good, easy, quick, and low calorie!

ESCAROLE SOUP WITH TURKEY MEATBALLS

2 servings
Source: Ground Turkey Greats

for soup

1 onion, chopped fine

1 teaspoon **chopped fresh rosemary leaves**

crumbled

1 tablespoon **olive oil**

½ lb. **escarole, (about 1/2 head), cut crosswise into 1/2 - inch strips,**

washed well and spun

dry, (about 6 cups,

packed)

3 ½ cups **low salt chicken broth**

¼ cup **orzo, (rice shaped pasta) or other small pasta**

for meatballs

¼ lb. **ground turkey**

3 tablespoons **fine fresh breadcrumbs**

1 large egg yolk

1 scallion, minced

1 tablespoon **freshly grated parmesan**

1 tablespoon **olive oil**

1 garlic clove, minced and mashed to a paste with 1/8 teaspoon salt

2 teaspoons **fresh lemon juice**

Make soup:

In a large heavy saucepan cook the onion and rosemary in oil over moderate heat, stirring, until onion is softened. Add escarole, stirring to coat with oil, and cook, covered, 1 minute. Add broth and orzo and simmer, partially covered, stirring occasionally, 10 minutes.

Make meatballs while soup simmers:

In a bowl combine well all meatball ingredients except oil and season with salt and pepper. Form mixture into meatballs about 1 inch in diameter. In a heavy 9-inch skillet heat oil over moderately high heat until hot but not smoking and brown meatballs about 3 minutes (meatballs will not be completely cooked through).

Add meatballs to soup and simmer, partially covered, 5 minutes. Stir in garlic paste, lemon juice, and salt and pepper to taste.

FRIED WON TONS

1 servings
Source: Ground Turkey Greats

1 lb. **won ton skins**

½ lb. **fresh ground pork**

½ lb. **fresh prawns**

4 dried mushrooms, soaked for 2 hours

8 water chestnuts, finely

2 stalks green onions, finely

2 small eggs, beaten

¼ teaspoon **pepper**

1 ½ teaspoons **salt**

Here are three won ton related recipes--fried won tons, won ton soup and a dip for the fried won tons. I have recipes for won ton dough too, if you want them. Personally, I find the won ton skins available in markets to be just fine and a lot less work! Yield: About 60 to 70.

Shell and devein prawns. Mince fine. Stem mushrooms and mince caps. Mix with prawns, pork, water chestnuts, green onions, half of the beaten eggs and all of the seasonings.

WRAPPING:

Place won ton squares on working surface so corners face up, down, left and right. Place 1 teaspoon filling in the center of each skin.

Dip a little of the beaten egg onto the bottom corner, bring top corner to meet bottom corner. Press to seal. Moisten left corner and bring right corner to meet it. Press to seal. [This should give you a little bundle that looks kinda like a nurses hat.]

FRYING:

Heat 4 cups oil in wok. Fry wrapped won ton until golden (about 2 minutes). Turn over once. Drain and serve hot.

DO-AHEAD NOTES:

Deep fry won ton, cool and freeze. To reheat, preheat oven to 350°F.

Place frozen won ton onto cookie sheets and heat for 12 to 15 minutes.

COMMENTS:

You may substitute ground turkey for meat in won ton filling.

However since turkey is drier and more bland than pork, add a few more water chestnuts and 1/4 tsp. monosodium glutamate to enhance flavor and texture.

GARDEN BURGERS

4 servings
Source: Ground Turkey Greats

egg white

¼ cup **fine dry bread crumbs**

¼ cup **finely shredded carrot**

¼ cup **finely chopped onion**

¼ cup **finely chopped green pepper**

½ teaspoon **salt**

⅛ teaspoon **pepper**

2 tablespoons **grated parmesan cheese**

1 lb. **ground turkey or lean beef**

1 medium tomato, sliced

In a large bowl combine egg white and bread crumbs.(if using beef, stir in 2 T water) Stir in carrot, onion, green pepper, salt, and pepper. Add Parmesan cheese and ground meat; mix well. Shape meat mixture into four 3/4" thick patties.

Spray a cold grill rack with Pam. Then place rack on grill.

Grill burgers on an uncovered grill directly over medium coals for 7 minutes. Turn and grill 8-11 minutes or till no pink remains. Place 1 tomato slice atop each burger and grill 1 minute more.

GREEK LASAGNA PIE

8 servings
Source: Ground Turkey Greats

¾ lbs. **ground turkey breast**

¼ cup **onion, chopped**

½ teaspoon **dried dill weed**

¼ teaspoon **dried oregano**

¼ teaspoon **garlic powder**

14 ½ ounces **canned diced tomatoes,**

drained

¼ teaspoon **salt**

⅛ teaspoon **pepper**

CHEESE MIXTURE 10 ounces frozen spinach -- chopped 15 ounces ricotta cheese (fat-free) 1 each Egg Beaters(r) 99% egg substitute 1/2 teaspoon garlic powder 1/4 teaspoon dried dill weed 10 each lasagna noodles -- uncooked SAUCE 8 ounces tomato sauce 1 teaspoon olive oil 1/2 teaspoon dried oregano 1/4 teaspoon sugar

Spray 9"cake pan.

In 2-qt. casserole, combine turkey, onion, 1/2 tsp. dill, 1/4 tsp. oregano and 1/4 tsp. garlic powder. Microwave HIGH for 5-7 min or until no longer pink. Drain. Add half of diced tomatoes, salt and pepper. Mix well and set aside.

Unwrap spinach and place on plate. Microwave HIGH for 4-6 min or until defrosted. Drain, pressing to remove excess moisture. In med. mixing bowl, combine spinach and remaining cheese mixture ingredients. Mix well. Set aside.

Prepare lasagna noodles as directed on package. Rinse and drain. Trim each cooked noodle to 8" in length. Arrange noodles, overlapping slightly, in spokelike fashion in 9-inch round cake dish.

Spoon cheese mixture in dish. Spread gently to make even layer. Top with meat mixture. Place ends of lasagna noodles over filling to enclose. Cover with plastic wrap. Microwave 70% (MED-HIGH) for 5-11 min or until center is 140°F. Let stand covered for 5 min.

Place remaining diced tomatoes and sauce ingredients in 1 qt. casserole. Microwave uncovered HIGH for 4-6 min or until sauce is hot and flavors are blended.

Invert pie on serving plate. Serve in wedges with sauce.

GREEN PAPAYA-TURKEY TUMBLE

1 servings
Source: Ground Turkey Greats

1 tablespoon **salad oil**

1 onion, peeled and chopped

1 lb. **ground turkey or ground lean pork**

1 tablespoon **curry powder**

5 ½ cups **diced green papaya**

¾ cup **fat-skimmed chicken broth**

3 tablespoons **chutney, chopped**

1 teaspoon **cornstarch**

Salt

12 iceberg or butter lettuce leaves

1. In a 10- to 12-inch frying pan over high heat, stir oil, onion, and turkey until meat is browned and crumbly, about 7 minutes.

2. Add curry powder; stir until fragrant, about 30 seconds. Add papaya, broth, and chutney. Cover and cook over medium heat, stirring occasionally, until papaya is tender when pierced, 5 to 7 minutes.

3. Mix cornstarch and 2 tablespoons water; stir into pan. Keep stirring until sauce boils, about 1 minute. Add salt to taste. Scrape into a bowl.

4. To eat, spoon turkey mixture into lettuce leaves and roll up.

NOTES: Serve as a first course or accompany with rice for a main dish. Garnish with green onion slivers.

MAKES: 6 first-course or 3 main-dish servings

GROUND TURKEY BURRITOS

8 servings
Source: Ground Turkey Greats

1 lb. **ground turkey or beef**

1 large onion, chopped

1 large green pepper, chopped

2 chiles serranos, (optional)

minced

1 clove garlic, minced

1 can refried beans

1 can chiles, chopped

¾ cups **picante sauce**

1 teaspoon **ground cumin**

½ teaspoon **oregano**

1 teaspoon **salt**

1 ds cayenne

1 cup **Monterey jack cheese -- shredded**

8 flour tortillas

Brown the turkey with onion, peppers and garlic. Drain excess fat. Add the remaining ingredients and simmer about 10 minutes. Let cool a bit so the mixture is a little firmer.

Warm the tortillas in the microwave or individually in a frying pan to soften. Put a big spoonful in the center of each tortilla, top with some cheese, and wrap, folding the ends within.

Optional additions: black beans, corn, more chiles, rice, whatever you like.

GROUND TURKEY IN LETTUCE CUPS

6 servings
Source: Ground Turkey Greats

2 tablespoons **soy sauce**

1 tablespoon **oyster sauce**

1 cup **hoisin sauce, divided**

2 teaspoons **cornstarch**

3 tablespoons **oil**

3 cloves **garlic, minced**

½ cup **diced white onion**

1 lb. **ground turkey - (to 1 1/4)**

1 teaspoon **coarse salt**

½ teaspoon **freshly-ground white pepper**

1 portabello mushroom - (to 1 1/2), diced

½ cup **diced red bell pepper**

½ cup **diced water chestnuts**

3 green onions, chopped

12 leaves Bibb lettuce

Combine the soy sauce, oyster sauce, 2 tablespoons of hoisin sauce and the cornstarch in a small bowl and set aside.

Heat the oil in a large skillet over high heat until very hot. Cook the garlic and white onion until soft, 30 seconds. Add the turkey, salt and pepper and cook the turkey until lightly browned though still slightly pink in the center, 2 to 3 minutes.

Stir in the mushrooms, bell pepper and water chestnuts. Add the sauce and continue cooking, stirring, until the sauce thickens and the turkey is cooked through, 2 to 3 minutes. Add the green onions and cook for 1 minute. Transfer the turkey mixture to a large serving bowl.

To serve, place 1/2 cup of the turkey into a lettuce leaf.

Spoon some of the remaining hoisin sauce on top, then roll the top and bottom edges of the leaf toward the middle while tucking in one of the sides to make a package similar to a burrito.

Repeat with the rest of the lettuce leaves and turkey mixture.

Serve the lettuce cups on individual plates or seal with a toothpick and serve on a platter.

This recipe yields 4 to 6 servings.

Each of 6 servings: 300 calories; 1,486 mg sodium; 52 mg cholesterol; 12 grams fat; 2 grams saturated fat; 26 grams carbohydrates; 22 grams protein; 2.47 grams fiber.

HONEY-MUSTARD TURKEY MEATBALLS

15 servings
Source: Ground Turkey Greats

1 lb. **ground turkey breast**

1 egg, lightly beaten

¾ cups **Ritz crackers, crushed**

½ cup **mozzarella cheese, part skim milk, shredded**

¼ cup **onion, chopped**

½ teaspoon **ground ginger**

6 tablespoons **Dijon mustard, divided**

1 ¼ cups **unsweetened pineapple juice**

¼ cup **chopped green bell pepper**

2 tablespoons **honey**

1 tablespoon **cornstarch**

¼ teaspoon **onion powder**

In a bowl, combine turkey, egg, cracker crumbs, cheese, onion, ginger and 3 tablespoons mustard. Form into 30 balls, 1 inch each.

Place in a greased 13-inch X 9-inch X 2-inch baking dish. Bake, uncovered, at 350°F for 20 - 25 minutes or until juices run clear.

In a saucepan, combine pineapple juice, green pepper, honey, cornstarch and onion powder; bring to a boil, stirring constantly. Cook and stir 2 minutes more; reduce heat. Stir in remaining mustard until smooth. Brush meatballs with about 1/4 cup sauce and return to the oven for 10 minutes. Serve remaining sauce as a dip for meatballs. Serving Size: 3 meatballs.

Author Note: I serve these often during the holidays. It's nice to have a turkey meatball that doesn't taste like you should have used beef. These meatballs can be prepare ahead and frozen, so you can treat even drop - in guests to a hot snack.

INDIAN SUMMER TURKEY CHILI

8 servings
Source: Ground Turkey Greats

3 tablespoons **extra-virgin olive oil, 2 turns of the pan**

2 ½ lbs. **ground turkey (85 percent lean) or ground turkey breast (99 percent lean), 2 packages**

4 tablespoons **dark chili powder, 2 palm fulls**

2 tablespoons **grill seasoning blend, any brand, 1 palm full**

1 tablespoon **cumin, 1/2 palm full**

2 tablespoons **Worcestershire sauce**

1 to 3 tablespoons **hot sauce, medium to extra-spicy**

1 large onion, quartered

2 large peppers, any color combination, red, green, purple, yellow or orange, chopped

½ bottle **beer (the alcohol cooks out), about 1 cup**

1 can **(14-ounce) tomato sauce**

½ cup **smoky barbecue sauce**

2 cups **corn kernels, optional**

Heat a pot over medium to medium high heat. Add extra-virgin olive oil, 3 turns of the pan, and the turkey meat. Season the meat with: chili powder, grill seasoning, cumin, Worcestershire and hot sauce. Break up the meat with the back of a wooden spoon into small crumbles.

Chop the onion, reserving 1/4 of it for topping the chili. Brown meat 5 minutes, then add onions and chopped bell peppers and cook 10 minutes more. Add beer and deglaze the pan, scraping up the drippings and cooking off the alcohol. Add tomato sauce and barbecue sauce and bring to a bubble. It using corn kernels add them now. Let chili simmer 10 minutes. Adjust seasonings and heat level to your taste. Remove from heat and serve.

- Prep: 10 Minutes
- Cook: 25 Minutes

ITALIAN MEATBALLS WITH PEPPERS

4 servings
Source: Ground Turkey Greats

1 lb. **ground turkey**

¼ cup **minced onion**

1 teaspoon **Italian seasoning**

¼ teaspoon **salt**

1 tablespoon **olive oil**

1 cup **cubed red pepper**

1 cup **cubed yellow pepper**

1 cup **thickly**

sliced fresh mushrooms

1 clove garlic, minced

1 chicken flavor bouillon cube

1 can evaporated skim milk

4 teaspoons **all purpose flour**

2 cups **hot cooked rice mixed with 3 T. parsley**

Italian parsley sprigs, optional

In large bowl, combine turkey, onion, Italian seasoning, and salt. Form into 16 meatballs. In 10 inch non-stick skillet, heat oil. Over medium high heat, brown meatballs; reduce heat and cook approximately 15 minutes or until done.

Remove meatballs and keep warm. Using drippings in skillet, saute peppers, mushrooms and garlic with bouillon cube for 2 to 3 minutes. In small bowl, gradually whisk evaporated skim milk into flour.

Add to skillet; cook over medium heat, stirring constantly, until sauce thickens slightly. Reduce heat; cover and simmer 5 minutes or until peppers are tender, stirring occasionally. Add meatballs; heat. Serve over cooked parsley-rice. Garnish with Italian parsley, if desired.

ITALIAN STUFFED MEATLOAF

30 servings
Source: Ground Turkey Greats

10 lbs. **Ground turkey or chicken**

10 lbs. **Ground lean beef**

6 tablespoons **Worcestershire sauce**

5 tablespoons **Prepared horseradish**

3 package StoveTop stuffing mix

1 cn Tomato sauce, 29 oz

1 cn Diced tomatoes

& green chili

2 cn Spaghetti sauce, 26.5 oz

6 teaspoons **Dried dill**

2 teaspoons **Dried tarragon**

6 teaspoons **Dried basil**

5 teaspoons **Dried oregano**

6 **Eggs, slightly beaten**

3 **Onions, diced**

1 cup **Parmesan cheese, grated**

4 teaspoons **Garlic pepper**

6 cups **Shredded mozzarella cheese**

1 **Diced zucchini squash**

1 **cn Pitted olives**

2 **cn Mushrooms**

Mix ground meat, stuffing mixes, 1 can spaghetti sauce, chopped onions, parmesan cheese, eggs, Worcestershire sauce, basil, oregano, dill, tarragon, diced tomatoes with green chilies, horseradish, garlic pepper, and tomato sauce.

Put half of mixture into greased roasting pan. Combine zucchini squash, mushrooms, olives and half of mozzarella cheese into a mixture and place on top of meat mixture. Place other half of reserved meat mixture on top of stuffing-filled bottom and seal edges.

Add remainder of shredded mozzarella cheese and second can of spaghetti sauce to top and bake in 350°F oven for about 1 1/2 hour, or until done. Add extra mozzarella cheese and sliced olives to top of loaf before serving!

JALEPENO BURGERS

4 servings
Source: Ground Turkey Greats

1 pound **ground turkey, or chicken or lean beef**

1 large **egg yolk**

1 smalll **jalapeno, seeded and chopped**

3 teaspoons **minced garlic**

2 teaspoons **worcestershire sauce**

2 tablespoons **tomato paste**

2 ounces **2% Monterey Jack Cheese, or other cheese about 1/2 cup**

4 each **whole-wheat hamburger buns, lightly toasted**

In a large bowl, stir meat, egg yolk, jalapeno, garlic, worcestershire, and tomato paste. Form mixture into 4 equal patties, about 3/4 inch thick.

Lightly coat large non-stick skillet with cooking spray and heat to medium high. Add burgers and cook until done, about 5 minutes per side. Top with cheese and cook until cheese melts, about one minute more.

- Prep: 10 Minutes
- Cook: 12 Minutes

JERK TURKEY BURGER

4 servings
Source: Ground Turkey Greats

1 lb. **ground turkey**

¼ cup **Jerk Seasoning, see below**

vegetable oil, for pan

4 slices Muenster cheese, (optional)

4 hamburger buns, lightly toasted

Sliced tomato, (optional)

Sliced mango, (optional)

Sliced white onion, (optional)

=== JERK SEASONING ===

2 bunches scallions, trimmed, and

finely chopped

4 teaspoons **ground allspice**

1 tablespoon **freshly-ground black pepper**

1 ½ teaspoons **coarse salt**

2 large garlic cloves, finely chopped

1 Scotch bonnet pepper, seeded, and

finely chopped

1 teaspoon **thyme leaves**

For the Jerk Seasoning: In a medium bowl, add all ingredients, and mix to combine. The seasoning can be refrigerated in an airtight container for up to 2 weeks. (Makes 1 cup).

Place turkey and jerk seasoning in a medium bowl, and stir to combine. Form into four patties.

Heat a grill pan or a grill to medium high. Lightly brush with oil. Grill until cooked through, about 8 minutes per side on grill pan or 7 minutes per side on grill.

If desired, place one slice of cheese on each burger for the last minute of cooking. Serve on toasted buns with sliced tomato, mango, and onion.

This recipe yields 4 servings.

Comments: When handling the Scotch bonnet pepper, protect your skin with latex or rubber gloves.

JERKY TURKEY BURGERS WITH PAPAYA SALSA

4 servings
Source: Ground Turkey Greats

1 ⅓ lbs. **ground turkey breast**

= (the average weight of 1 package)

1 clove **garlic, minced**

2 scallions, thinly sliced

1 serrano or jalapeno pepper, seeded, minced

1 piece ginger root - (abt 1"), grated

2 teaspoons **chopped fresh thyme leaves**

1 teaspoon **allspice**

½ teaspoon **freshly-grated or ground nutmeg**

1 teaspoon **coarsely-ground black pepper**

Coarse salt, to taste

Extra-virgin olive oil, for drizzling

= (or vegetable oil)

1 ripe lime, juiced

4 bib or green leaf lettuce leaves

4 Kaiser rolls, split

= (crusty plain or cornmeal dusted)

=== PAPAYA SALSA ===

1 large ripe papaya, seeded, peeled,

and diced

½ red bell pepper, seeded, diced

¼ red onion, finely chopped

1 serrano or jalapeno pepper, seeded, and

finely chopped

2 tablespoons **fresh cilantro leaves**

1 navel orange, juiced

Coarse salt, to taste

Preheat a large nonstick skillet, indoor grill pan or tabletop grill to medium-high heat. Combine the turkey, garlic, scallions, ginger, thyme, allspice, nutmeg, salt and pepper in a medium bowl.

Form mixture into 4 large patties no more than 1-inch thick. Drizzle the patties with a touch of oil. Place patties in a hot pan or on a hot grill and cook 6 minutes on each side.

Squeeze the juice of 1 ripe lime over the patties before removing them from the heat. Place the cooked patties on bun bottoms and top with lettuce leaves.

Combine the papaya, red bell pepper, red onion, serrano or jalapeno, cilantro and orange juice in a bowl. Season salsa with salt, to your taste.

Pile salsa on top of the lettuce resting on cooked patties and add bun tops to the burgers. This recipe yields 4 servings.

MAKE YOUR OWN TACOS BAR

10 servings
Source: Ground Turkey Greats

10 super-size taco shells, warmed to

directions on package

=== CHIPOTLE TURKEY TACO FILLING ===

1 tablespoon **extra-virgin olive oil**

1 ⅓ lbs. **ground turkey breast**

= (the average weight of 1 package)

1 small onion, chopped

2 cloves **garlic, chopped**

2 chipotles in adobo sauce, chopped

1 cup **tomato sauce**

1 tablespoon **chili powder - (rounded)**

Salt, to taste

½ cup **water**

=== PORK AND BELL PEPPER FILLING ===

1 tablespoon **extra-virgin olive oil**

1 ⅓ lbs. **ground pork**

½ red bell pepper, chopped

½ yellow bell pepper, chopped

1 small green bell pepper, chopped

1 tablespoon **ground cumin**

Several drops cayenne pepper sauce, to taste

½ teaspoon **allspice**

Salt, to taste

Freshly-ground black pepper, to taste

½ cup **water**

=== TOPPINGS AND SIDES ===

1 ½ cups **shredded cheddar or smoked cheddar, (abt 1/2 lb)**

1 ½ cups **shredded Monterey Pepper Jack cheese, (abt 1/2 lb)**

Shredded Romaine lettuce - (2 hearts)

6 scallions, chopped

Diced red plum tomatoes

Taco sauce, any brand

=== YELLOW PICO DE GALLO ===

3 yellow vine ripe tomatoes, seeded, diced

2 small jalapeno peppers, seeded, chopped

1 small white onion, chopped

3 tablespoons **chopped fresh cilantro leaves**

Coarse salt, to taste

Chipotle Turkey Taco Filling: In a small skillet preheated over medium-high heat, add oil and turkey breast meat. Brown meat 2 or 3 minutes, then add onions and garlic. Cook onions and meat together for another 3 to 5 minutes. Stir in chipotles, chili powder and tomato sauce. Season your filling with salt to your taste. Stir 1/2 cup water into your filling. Reduce heat to medium-low and simmer until ready to serve.

Pork and Bell Pepper Filling: Heat a small to medium skillet over medium-high heat. Add oil and pork to hot pan. Break up pork as it browns, 2 to 3 minutes. Add peppers to the pork and season mixture with cumin, cayenne sauce, allspice, salt and pepper. Reduce heat to moderate and cook filling 5 minutes longer. Add 1/2 cup water to the pork. Reduce heat to low to keep filling warm.

Yellow Pico de Gallo: Combine all Pico de Gallo ingredients in a small bowl and serve.

To assemble bar, arrange taco shells next to the stove top. Serve the fillings from the skillets they were cooked in. Place toppings in small dishes on opposite side of the stove top. Tex Mex Red Beans And Rice (see recipe) or store bought refried beans make a great side dish.

This recipe yields 10 tacos.

MEATLOAF

8 servings
Source: Ground Turkey Greats

- **1** can **(6 oz.) no-salt added tomato paste**
- ½ cup **dry red wine**
- ½ cup **water**
- **1** teaspoon **minced garlic**
- ½ teaspoon **dried basil leaves**
- ½ teaspoon **dried oregano leaves**
- ¼ teaspoon **salt**
- **16** ounces **ground turkey breast**
- ¼ cup **shredded zucchini**
- ¼ cup **cholesterol-free egg substitute or 2 egg w**

Preheat oven to 350 degrees. Combine tomato paste, wine, water, garlic, basil, oregano and salt in small saucepan. Bring to boil; reduce heat to low. Simmer, uncovered, 15 minutes. Set aside.

Combine turkey, zucchini, egg substitute and 1/2 cup reserved tomato mixture in large bowl. Mix well. Shape into loaf; place into ungreased 9x5x3-inch loaf pan.

Bake 45 minutes. Discard any drippings. Pour 1/2 cup remaining tomato mixture over top of loaf. Bake an additional 15 minutes. Place on serving platter. Cool 10 minutes before slicing. Garnish as desired. Makes 8 servings.

MINI CHEESEBURGER SALAD WITH YELLOW MUSTARD VINAIGRETTE

4 servings
Source: Ground Turkey Greats

1 ½ lbs. **ground sirloin or ground turkey**

¼ cup **finely-chopped onion**

1 tablespoon **Worcestershire sauce**

2 teaspoons **steak seasoning blend**

= **(or coarse salt and ground black pepper)**

Extra-virgin olive oil, for drizzling

¾ lbs. **brick sharp Cheddar***

= **(Cabot brand or Cracker Barrel brand**

recommended)

3 large romaine lettuce hearts

1 cup **sliced pickles, drained**

= **(choose from sweet, half-sour or**

dill varieties)

1 cup **cherry or grape tomatoes**

=== **DRESSING** ===

3 tablespoons **yellow mustard**

= **(French's brand recommended)**

2 tablespoons **apple cider vinegar**

½ cup **extra-virgin olive oil**

2 tablespoons **finely-chopped chives**

2 tablespoons **drained salad pimentos**

= (or 1/4 small red bell pepper, finely chopped)

* There are many flavors of sharp Cheddar out in today's markets to choose from, so go plain or go wild! Among the choices out there in sharp cheddars: 5-peppercorn, smoked, dill, garlic and herb, roasted garlic, horseradish, chipotle, habanero, jalapeno -- on and on!

Preheat a grill pan or a large nonstick skillet over medium-high heat or, preheat outdoor grill.

Combine the meat with onion, Worcestershire and steak seasoning or salt and pepper. Form 2-inch meatballs, then flatten them into patties. Drizzle formed mini patties with extra-virgin olive oil to keep them from sticking to cooking surface.

Slice the brick of cheese into 1/4-inch pieces. Place patties into a preheated pan or grill pan or arrange on outdoor grill. Cook the mini burgers for 3 minutes on each side then add cheese to melt over patties. On outdoor grill, close the lid to melt cheese. In a skillet or on a grill pan, tent the mini cheeseburgers loosely with foil to melt cheese.

Coarsely chop romaine and combine with sliced pickles and halved cherry or grape tomatoes.

Whisk together the mustard and cider vinegar. Stream in the extra-virgin olive oil. Add the chopped chives and pimentos, stir to combine

Arrange mini cheeseburgers on salad and drizzle prepared yellow mustard over the completed dish.

This recipe yields 4 servings.

Chapter 2
N-Z

PORK AND BEANS CASSEROLE

1 servings
Source: Ground Turkey Greats

1 lb. **ground turkey**

1 onion

32 ounces **baked beans**

½ cup **brown sugar**

½ tablespoon **salt**

1 tablespoon **yellow mustard**

8 ounces **tomato sauce**

1 tablespoon **Worcestershire sauce**

Chop onion. Cook turkey until it changes color; breaking apart with a fork (about 3 minutes). Add onion and heat thoroughly. Add remaining ingredients and heat until mixture begins to simmer. Put in a 2-quart casserole; cover. Bake in 350°F. oven 30 minutes. Serves 6. Freezes well.

PORTUGUESE RICE

8 servings
Source: Ground Turkey Greats

2 teaspoons **olive oil**

¼ teaspoon **salt**

1 ¼ cups **brown rice**

2 lbs. **lean ground turkey**

1 medium onion, chopped

2 cloves garlic, finely

2 28 oz cans peeled tomatoes, chopped with juice

1 16 oz ca tomato sauce

1 teaspoon **hot red pepper sauce, or to**

½ teaspoon **dried oregano**

½ teaspoon **black pepper**

In a medium saucepan, bring cups water, the oil, and salt to a boil over high heat. Add the brown rice, reduce the heat to low, and simmer covered for about 50 minutes, until the rice is tender. Drain the rice if necessary, and set aside.

Meanwhile in a large nonstick skillet, cook the ground turkey, chopped onion, and garlic over medium heat for about 7 minutes, stirring occasionally, until the turkey loses its pink color. Stir in the tomatoes and their juice, tomato sauce, hot pepper sauce, oregano, and black pepper.

Bring to a simmer, reduce the heat to low, and cook, uncovered, for about 45 minutes. Stir in the cooked brown rice, simmer an additional 5 minutes, and serve immediately.

RANCHO DAGWOOD

1 servings
Source: Ground Turkey Greats

1 loaf (1 lb.) French sourdough bread

6 slices mozzarella or provolone cheese, thinly sliced

¾ lbs. **ground lean ground turkey**

¼ lb. **mushrooms, sliced**

½ teaspoon **dried oregano**

1 cup **purchased marinara sauce or pizza sauce**

1 can **sliced ripe olives, (21/4 oz.) drained**

1 cup **thinly sliced green onions**

Salt and pepper

3 tablespoons **grated parmesan cheese**

1. Split loaf in half horizontally. Scoop out soft centers, making top and bottom bread shells about 1/2 inch thick. Reserve centers for another use. Set bread shells, cupped side up, on a 12- by 15-inch baking sheet. Bake in a 400° oven until bread is toasted, about 8 minutes.

2. Line bread shell cavities with mozzarella, overlapping slices as needed, and draping onto the rim of the bread.

3. In a 10- to 12-inch nonstick frying pan over high heat, frequently stir meat, mushrooms, and oregano until meat is browned and crumbly, 7 to 8 minutes. Add half the marinara sauce, half the olives, 3/4 cup onions, and salt and pepper to taste.

4. Fill bread shells equally with meat mixture. Top meat filling with remaining marinara sauce, olives, and onions. Sprinkle with parmesan.

5. Bake in a 400° oven until hot throughout, 10 to 15 minutes. Cut crosswise into 2- to 3-inch sections.

RIGATONI WITH GROUND TURKEY

1 servings
Source: Ground Turkey Greats

1 lb. **ground turkey**

⅓ cup **onion, chopped**

2 tablespoons **parsley, minced**

1 lb. **mushrooms, sliced**

1 ounce **porcini mushrooms --**

rehydrate

save water

½ cup **tomatoes, chopped**

rigatoni, cooked al dente

toasted breadcrumbs

⅓ cup **parmesan cheese**

⅔ cups **b?chamel sauce**

1 tablespoon **olive oil**

2 tablespoons **flour**

1 cup **milk**

salt and pepper

Saute turkey; add onions, parsley, mushrooms, tomatoes and porcinis with their juice. Cook until meat is done and onions are tender. Toss pasta with sauce. Put in a baking dish.

Top with Bechamel Sauce, breadcrumbs and Parmesan. Bake 400°F for 15 minutes.

BECHAMEL SAUCE-Cook flour in oil until smooth. Add milk, salt and pepper. Cook until thick.

SAVORY TURKEY MEATLOAF FLORENTINE

8 servings
Source: Ground Turkey Greats

1 ½ lbs. **ground turkey**

½ cup **cream of wheat**

½ cup **egg substitute**

½ cup **ketchup**

1 clove garlic, minced

1 teaspoon **dried basil leaves**

1 10 oz pkg chopped spinach, thawed, drained

½ cup **chopped red pepper**

¼ cup **minced onion**

1 tablespoon **country-style Dijon mustard**

1 tablespoon **honey**

In large bowl, thoroughly combine turkey, cereal, egg substitute, ketchup, garlic and basil. Stir in spinach, pepper and onion. Shape into 9x4-inch loaf.

Place in greased 13x9x2-inch baking pan. Bake at 350°F for 45 minutes. Blend mustard and honey; brush over meatloaf.

Bake 15-25 minutes more or until internal temperature reaches 165F.

Let stand 10 minutes before slicing.

SLOPPY TURKEY SPUDS

4 servings
Source: Ground Turkey Greats

4 potatoes, (10 ounces each)

12 ounces **ground turkey**

1 medium onion, chopped

1 medium green bell pepper, chopped

1 cup **sliced mushrooms**

1 jar or can marinara sauce, or- other vegetarian sp spaghetti sauce, - (14 or 15 ounces)

salt and pepper, to taste

¼ cup **chopped parsley**

¼ cup **grated parmesan cheese**

Pierce potatoes with tines of fork; microwave on HIGH 20 to 22 minutes until potatoes are fork-tender. Meanwhile, in large nonstick skillet over medium heat saute turkey until no longer pink, about 6 minutes.

Add onion, bell pepper and mushrooms; saute, stirring, 3 minutes.

Stir in marinara sauce; bring to boil, reduce heat, cover and simmer 10 minutes. Season with salt and pepper; stir in parsley. Place potatoes on 4 plates; split and fluff. Top potatoes with turkey mixture and cheese, dividing equally.

NOTE: Microwave cooking times are based on a 700-watt microwave. Adjust cooking times to your own oven.

SMOKY TURKEY SHEPHERD'S PIE

4 servings
Source: Ground Turkey Greats

3 large Idaho potatoes, peeled, cubed

Coarse salt, as needed

2 tablespoons **extra-virgin olive oil**

¼ lb. **smoky bacon or turkey bacon, chopped**

1 ⅓ lbs. **ground turkey breast**

1 tablespoon **smoked paprika**

= (may substitute 1 1/2 tspns each sweet

paprika and cumin combined)

Coarsely-ground black pepper, to taste

2 tablespoons **fresh thyme leaves - (5 or 6 sprigs)**

1 medium onion, chopped

2 carrots, peeled, diced

3 celery ribs from the heart, chopped

1 small red bell pepper, seeded, chopped

2 cups **frozen peas**

2 tablespoons **all-purpose flour**

2 cups **chicken broth**

1 cup **sour cream, divided**

3 tablespoons **butter**

1 large egg, beaten

10 blades fresh chives - (to 12), chopped or snipped

Bring a medium pot of water to a boil, salt it, and cook the potatoes until tender, 12 to 15 minutes.

Heat a deep, large skillet over medium-high heat. Add olive oil, 2 turns of the pan, to the skillet. Add bacon and brown it up, then add ground turkey to the pan and break it up. Season the turkey with smoked paprika, salt and pepper, and thyme. When turkey browns up, add: onions, carrots, celery. Season the veggies with salt and pepper. Cook 5 minutes, then add red pepper and peas cook another 2 minutes. Stir in flour and cook flour 2 minutes. Whisk in broth and combine. Add 1/2 cup of sour cream and combine. Simmer mixture over low heat.

Preheat your broiler to high.

When potatoes are tender, add a ladle of cooking water to the egg. Drain potatoes and return to the warm pot to dry them out a little. Add remaining 1/2 cup sour cream, butter, half of the chives, and salt and pepper. Smash and mash the potatoes, mashing in the beaten, tempered egg. If the potatoes are too tight, mix in a splash of milk.

Pour turkey mixture into a medium casserole dish. Top turkey with an even layer of smashed potatoes and place casserole 5 inches from hot broiler. Broil the potatoes until golden at edges and remove the casserole from the oven. Garnish the casserole with the remaining chives and a sprinkle of smoked paprika.

This recipe yields 4 servings.

SOUTHWEST TURKEY BURGERS

4 servings
Source: Ground Turkey Greats

8 slices turkey bacon

= **(or turkey bacon with black pepper or**

applewood smoked bacon)

1 ⅓ lbs. **ground turkey breast**

= **(the average weight of 1 package)**

2 cloves **garlic, finely chopped**

1 large shallot or 1/4 red onion, finely chopped

2 tablespoons **chopped fresh thyme leaves**

= **(or 1 tspn dried thyme leaves)**

2 tablespoons **chopped fresh cilantro leaves, (optional)**

= **(parsley may be substituted)**

½ small green, red, or yellow bell pepper, seeded, chopped fine

1 serrano or jalape“o pepper, seeded, chopped fine

2 teaspoons **ground cumin**

1 teaspoon **cayenne hot sauce - (to 2)**

= **(Tabasco recommended)**

2 teaspoons **grill seasoning blend**

= **(Montreal Steak Seasoning by McCormick**

recommended)

Vegetable oil or olive oil, for drizzling

½ lb. **deli-sliced pepper jack cheese**

4 crusty kaiser rolls, split

1 cup **sweet red pepper relish**

= **(pepper jelly may be substituted)**

Red leaf lettuce, as needed

Spicy O-Nuts, (see recipe)

Chop your garlic and veggies.

Cook bacon in a large nonstick skillet over medium-high heat until crisp. Wipe excess grease from pan and return skillet to heat.

While bacon cooks, combine turkey meat, garlic, shallot or onion, thyme, cilantro or parsley, bell pepper, serrano or jalapeno pepper, cumin, hot pepper sauce, grill seasoning or salt and pepper. Divide mixture into 4 equal mounds then form meat into patties.

Drizzle patties with vegetable oil to coat. Cook in skillet over medium high heat for 5 to 6 minutes on each side. Place sliced cheese over the patties in the last 2 minutes of cooking, use 1 or 2 slices for each patty, as you like.

Pile cooked cheeseburgers into buns. Spread sweet relish or jelly on bun tops and set red leaf lettuce into place, using the relish or jelly as glue. Top cheeseburgers with 2 slices of cooked, crisp bacon or turkey bacon and lettuce. Then serve with tortilla chips, tossed salad and/or Spicy O-nuts.

This recipe yields 4 servings.

SPAGHETTI DISH

8 servings
Source: Ground Turkey Greats

2 cups **angel hair pasta, cooked**

1 tablespoon **margarine, melted**

1 cup **egg white**

¼ cup **parmesan cheese**

1 cup **fat-free cottage cheese**

FILLING

1 lb. **ground turkey, cooked**

1 cup **onions, chopped**

1 cup **bell peppers, chopped**

1 8 oz can tomato sauce

3 teaspoons **oregano**

3 teaspoons **basil**

2 teaspoons **salt**

1 cup **mozzarella cheese -- shredded**

Preheat oven at 350. Prepare 13 x 9 x 2" pan with cooking spray. To prepare crust, cook pasta in a saucepan with a large amount of boiling water for 10 to 12 minutes or until tender.

Drain well. Return to saucepan and stir margarine, egg whites, and Parmesan cheese into hot pasta. Press spaghetti mixture onto bottom of prepared pan. Spread cottage cheese over crust.

To prepare filling, cook turkey, onion, and peppers in a skillet until meat is no longer pink. Drain off fat, if needed. Stir in tomato sauce, oregano, basil, and salt. Spread meat mixture over cottage cheese. Sprinkle mozzarella cheese over meat mixture. Bake for 25 minutes.

SPAGHETTI SAUCE WITH TURKEY MEATBALLS

6 servings
Source: Ground Turkey Greats

1 cup **onion, chopped**

2 teaspoons **Italian seasoning, crushed**

1 cup **green pepper, coarsely**

½ teaspoon **sugar**

chopped

½ teaspoon **garlic powder**

½ cup **carrot, coarsely chopped**

½ teaspoon **salt**

½ cup **celery, sliced**

12 ounces **spaghetti or mostaccioli**

2 16 oz can tomatoes, cut up

cooked and drained

1 6 oz can tomato paste, (2/3 cup) -turkey meatballs---

Ground Turkey Greats

1 egg, beaten

½ teaspoon **salt**

2 tablespoons **low-fat milk**

⅛ teaspoon **pepper**

¼ cup **bread crumbs, fine**

1 lb. **ground turkey**

½ teaspoon **Italian seasoning**

For Sauce:

Cook onion, green pepper, carrot, and celery in a covered 4 1/2qt Dutch oven in a small amount of boiling water for 4 minutes or till tender. Drain.

Stir in undrained canned tomatoes, tomato paste, Italian seasoning, sugar, garlic powder, and salt.

Bring to boiling; reduce heat.

Add meatballs; cover and simmer for 30 minutes.

If necessary, uncover and simmer for 10 to 15 minutes more or to desired consistency, stirring occasionally.

Serve over hot cooked pasta.

For Meatballs: In a medium bowl, combine all ingredients, except the turkey.

Mix well and add the ground turkey; mix well.

With wet hands, shape meat into 24 - 1 inch balls.

Spray a 13x9x2 inch baking pan with nonstick spray.

Place meatballs in prepared pan.

Bake in a 375°F oven for 20 minutes or till no pink remains; drain.

SPAGHETTI WITH TURKEY-BLACK BEAN CHILI

6 servings
Source: Ground Turkey Greats

1 lb. **spaghetti**

or linguine, uncooked

2 tablespoons **vegetable oil, divided**

12 ounces **ground turkey**

1 **small onion, peeled and finely diced**

1 **jalapeno, cored and thinly sliced**

1 tablespoon **chili powder**

1 teaspoon **cumin**

2 **garlic cloves, finely chopped**

16 ounces **canned black beans, rinsed and drained**

15 ounces **canned crushed tomatoes**

2 tablespoons **chopped fresh cilantro**

2 cups **water**

Heat the oil in a large, deep skillet over medium heat. Crumble the turkey into the skillet. Cook, stirring to break up the turkey, until the liquid is evaporated from the skillet and the turkey begins to brown, about 5 minutes. Add the onion, jalapeno, chili powder, cumin and garlic and cook until the onion is softened, about 5 minutes. Add the beans, tomatoes, cilantro and water. Heat to boiling, reduce the heat and simmer, covered, 15 minutes. Add salt and pepper to taste. (The chili can be made up to one day in advance.)

Prepare pasta according to package directions. Drain the pasta and return it to the pot. Add the chili and stir over medium heat until the sauce is simmering and the pasta is coated with sauce. Divide among bowls and serve immediately.

Each serving provides: 834 Calories; 41.6 g Protein; 131 g Carbohydrates; 15.5 g Fat; 57.8 mg Cholesterol; 197 mg Sodium. Calories from Fat: 17%.

SPICY TURKEY BURGERS

4 servings
Source: Ground Turkey Greats

1 lb. **ground turkey**

1 teaspoon **garlic powder**

1 teaspoon **cayenne pepper**

½ teaspoon **cumin**

1 teaspoon **black pepper**

Preheat oven to broil. Spray a broiler pan with no-stick cooking spray.

Combine all ingredients in a mixing bowl and mix well. Shape into 4 patties. Place on broiler pan and broil for 5 minutes on each side. Serve on hamburger buns. Serves 4.

SWEET AND SOUR MEATBALLS - 1

1 servings
Source: Ground Turkey Greats

1 lb. **ground beef, or ground turkey**

¾ cups **steak sauce**

½ cup **bread crumbs**

1 egg, beaten

1 8 oz can pineapple chunks, with juice

1 medium green bell pepper, diced

6 mushrooms, diced

Mix the above ingredients together. However, only mix 1/2 cup steak sauce to ground beef mixture.

Leave the other 1/4 cup of steak sauce on side and mix w/drained pineapple juice. Shape into meatballs.

Dip meatballs into steak sauce mixture.

Either grill and brush sauce over frequently or broil for 10 to 15 minutes. Can add cherry tomatoes and other veggies to kabobs.

Here's a recipe great for kabobs and to get us ready for barbecues.

SWEET AND SPICY TURKEY LOAF

6 servings
Source: Ground Turkey Greats

1 lb. **ground turkey**

1 cup **finely chopped onion**

⅔ cups **herb-seasoned**

stuffing mix crushed

2 tablespoons **dried parsley flakes**

1 teaspoon **salt**

1 teaspoon **poultry seasoning**

½ teaspoon **black pepper**

¼ teaspoon **dried sage**

vegetable cooking spray

½ cup **whole cranberry sauce**

¼ cup **jalapeno jelly**

2 tablespoons **chopped walnuts toasted**

In medium bowl combine turkey, onion, stuffing mix, parsley, salt, poultry seasoning, pepper, and sage. Mix well.

In (9-inch diameter) pie plate, sprayed with vegetable oil, shape mixture into a round loaf approximately 7 inches in diameter.

Bake at 350°F for 45 to 60 minutes or until meat thermometer, inserted in center, registers 160 to 165°F and juices run clear.

In small saucepan, over low heat, combine cranberry sauce and jelly. Cook and stir 5 to 7 minutes or until sauce is smooth and bubbly; stir in walnuts.

To serve, top meatloaf with sauce and slice.

SZECHUAN-STYLE CHICKEN AND BROCCOLI

4 servings
Source: Ground Turkey Greats

2 chicken breasts*, boneless, skinless

⅓ cup **pace picante sauce**

20 garlic, minced

2 tablespoons **soy sauce**

1 tablespoon **ginger, shredded**

1 tablespoon **water**

1 tablespoon **cornstarch**

1 ½ cups **broccoli flowerets**

½ teaspoon **sugar**

1 red pepper

3 tablespoons **vegetable oil**

1 onion, thin wedges

* We use much less meat than this; either 1 whole chicken breast or 1/2 lb. ground turkey or ground chicken.

Cut chicken into 1-inch cubes. Combine picante sauce, soy sauce, water, cornstarch and sugar in small bowl; set aside. Heat 2 T. of the oil in wok or large skillet over medium high heat. Add chicken and stir-fry 3 to 4 minutes or until cooked through. Remove with slotted spoon. Add remaining oil onion, garlic and ginger to skillet; stir-fry 30 seconds. Add broccoli and peppers; stir-fry 3 minutes or until vegetables are crisp-tender. Add chicken and picante sauce mixture; stir-fry about 1 minute or until sauce thickens.

I don't cook the meat and vegetables separately. It takes a little longer, but there are less dishes to wash and you only need 2 T. oil. I cook the garlic and ginger for a few seconds before throwing the meat in. I cook the meat for 20 or 30 seconds, and then throw in the vegetables one at a one at a time, stirring 5 or 6 seconds between each addition.

I cook everything for 5 or 6 minutes, stirring, of course. Then I pull everything up on the sides of the wok and pour the sauce in the center, stirring the sauce until thickened. Then I stir everything together for a minute or two. It's done. I use high on my stove when cooking with my wok on a fire-ring. This is easy and delicious and lower in sodium than many of the bottled sauces.

TACO POCKETS

4 servings
Source: Ground Turkey Greats

1 ⅓ lbs. **ground sirloin or ground turkey breast**

1 **small onion, finely chopped**

2 cloves **garlic, chopped**

1 tablespoon **ground cumin**

1 tablespoon **dark chili powder**

1 teaspoon **cayenne pepper sauce**

1 teaspoon **coarse salt**

1 tablespoon **vegetable oil**

= (1 turn around the pan)

4 **soft flour tortillas - (12" dia)**

1 cup **mild taco sauce**

1 **romaine lettuce heart, shredded**

2 **small plum tomatoes, seeded, chopped**

2 cups **shredded monterey jack**

=== ACCOMPANIMENTS ===

Cut fresh seasonal vegetable pieces and

strips

Assorted organic tortillas

= (like blue corn, red corn or

black bean)

So Mild Salsa

= (for dipping chips and vegetables)

Combine ground meat with onion, garlic, spices, and salt and form 4 patties. Pan fry patties in 1 tablespoon oil over medium-high heat for 7 minutes on each side.

To make a taco pocket, blister a flour tortilla on a hot griddle pan for 30 seconds on each side. Place tortilla on dinner plate and spread surface with 1/4 cup mild taco sauce. Pile shredded lettuce, tomatoes and a handful of cheese in center of tortilla. Top veggies and cheese with cooked taco burger patty and wrap tortilla up and over patty on all four sides. Turn square pouch over and cut from corner to corner, making 2 taco pockets that will not crumble and drip like traditional tacos.

Serve taco pockets with cut fresh seasonal veggies, assorted tortilla chips and So Mild Salsa for dipping.

This recipe yields 4 servings.

TEX-MEX TURKEY STEW

6 servings
Source: Ground Turkey Greats

1 tablespoon **oil**

1 lb. **ground turkey**

1 **1-¾** ounces **Package taco seasoning**

1 cup **canned diced tomatoes**

with juices

1 cup **whole kernel corn**

1 Small green chili pepper

seeded and chopped

½ cup **water**

2 cups **red, yellow, orange or green peppers chopped**

1 cup **cubed potatoes cooked**

1 cup **dark red kidney beans**

rinsed and drained well

¼ teaspoon **salt**

½ teaspoon **pepper**

6 Medium to Large red,

yellow, orange or green peppers halved and seeded

1 cup **dried bread crumbs buttered**

½ cup **Monterey cheese shredded**

Over medium heat, heat oil in a large fry pan. Add turkey and lightly brown, breaking turkey into medium size chunks.

Stir in taco seasoning mix and blend well.

Add next 4 ingredients; stir and cook for 5 minutes.

Add chopped peppers and potatoes; simmer covered for 3 minutes. Stir in drained kidney beans. Cover and reduce heat to warm.

Microwave pepper halves for 7 minutes, turning halfway through.

Fill pepper shells with turkey mixture, top with bread crumbs and cheese.

Broil about 4 inches from the heat source for 5 minutes to brown bread crumbs and melt cheese.

THAI TURKEY BITES

25 servings
Source: Ground Turkey Greats

¼ cup **boiling water**

3 tablespoons **brown sugar**

3 tablespoons **lime or lemon juice**

1 medium cucumber, cut in half

and cut into, 1/4 inch thick slice

½ **small onion, thinly sliced, halved and separated**

1 red or green chili

pepper, chopped fine

1 lb. **ground turkey**

4 teaspoons **fish or soy sauce**

1 tablespoon **red curry paste or**

1 teaspoon **chili powder**

and 1/2 oil

For sauce: In a mixing bowl combined water, brown sugar, and lime juice.

Stir till brown sugar dissolves. Add cucumber slices, onion, and chili pepper. Mix well. Cover and chill up to 3 days. In a mixing bowl, combine ground turkey, fish or soy sauce, and red curry paste. mix well. Shape turkey mixture into 1-inch meatballs; flatten slightly. Arrange meatballs in a microwave safe 8x8x2 inch baking dish. Cover dish loosely with waxed paper.

Micro-cook on 100% power for 5 to 7 minutes or till done, turning meatballs over and rotating dish a half-turn once.

To serve, place meatballs in a chafing dish over burner. Transfer sauce to serving bowl.

With a toothpick spear a cucumber slice, then a meatball. Dip in sauce. Makes 25 to 30 meatballs. Meatballs maybe frozen.

TRADITIONAL SPAGHETTI & MEATBALLS

6 servings
Source: Ground Turkey Greats

1 lb. **Spaghetti, Linguine or Thin Spaghetti, uncooked - Meatballs---**

4 slices white bread

½ cup **skim milk**

2 large egg whites

8 ounces **ground turkey**

8 ounces **extra lean ground beef**

¼ cup **grated Romano cheese**

1 tablespoon **minced fresh basil or**

1 teaspoon **dried basil**

1 teaspoon **minced fresh oregano**

or 1/2 tsp. dried oregano

½ teaspoon **salt**

¼ teaspoon **pepper**

--Sauce---

1 Basic Tomato Sauce

1 teaspoon **vegetable oil, divided**

Put the bread into a medium mixing bowl and pour the milk over it. Let sit 5 minutes. Add the egg whites, ground turkey, ground beef, Romano cheese, basil, oregano, salt and pepper. Knead the mixture with your hands until it is smooth. To prevent sticking, dip your hands into cool water before forming each meatball. Form mixture into 30 1 1/2-inch balls.

Pour the tomato sauce into a large, heavy-bottom saucepan and bring to a simmer over low heat. Warm 1/2 teaspoon vegetable oil in a large non-stick skillet. Add half the meatballs to the skillet and brown them on all sides.

Spoon the meatballs into the tomato sauce. Add the remaining 1/2 teaspoon vegetable oil to the skillet and brown the rest of the meatballs, then add them to the sauce. Simmer, stirring, for 20 minutes.

While sauce is simmering, prepare pasta according to package directions; drain. Transfer to a large serving bowl. Remove bay leaves from sauce; pour sauce over pasta and serve.

TURKEY AND MUSHROOM BURGERS

1 servings
Source: Ground Turkey Greats

1 egg white, (about 2 tbsp)

¼ cup **white wine, dry**

⅓ cup **soft French bread crumbs**

¼ teaspoon **salt**

1 lb. **ground turkey, (breast best)**

⅛ teaspoon **pepper**

¼ cup **shallots, finely chopped**

2 ounces **mushrooms, finely chopped**

cooking spray

In medium size bowl, beat egg white and wine until blended. Stir in crumbs, salt, pepper and shallots; then lightly mix in turkey and mushrooms. Shape turkey mixture into 6 patties, each about 1/2 inch thick.

Cook just like hamburgers either on the stovetop using non-stick spray on pan or on the grill (best!).

TURKEY AND WILD MUSHROOM MEAT LOAF PATTIES WITH PAN GRAVY

4 servings
Source: Ground Turkey Greats

3 tablespoons **extra-virgin olive oil**

8 cremini mushrooms (baby portobellos)*, chopped

8 shiitake mushrooms*, chopped

1 shallot, chopped

Salt, to taste

Freshly-ground black pepper, to taste

1 ⅓ lbs. **ground turkey**

= **(the average weight of 1 package)**

2 tablespoons **chopped fresh sage leaves**

1 tablespoon **Worcestershire sauce**

½ cup **Italian bread crumbs**

1 egg, beaten

2 tablespoons **butter**

2 tablespoons **all-purpose flour**

2 cups **chicken stock**

1 teaspoon **poultry seasoning**

* Clean mushrooms with a damp cloth. Do not run directly under water.

Heat a nonstick skillet over medium-high heat. Add 2 tablespoons of the oil. Add chopped mushrooms and shallots and season with salt and pepper. Saute mushrooms 5 or 6 minutes until dark and tender. Remove from heat. Transfer mushrooms to a bowl and return pan to stove top to preheat to cook patties.

Add turkey to the mushroom mixture. Make a well in the center of the meat. Add sage, Worcestershire sauce, bread crumbs and beaten egg and season with salt and pepper. Mix turkey meat loaf and make a small 1-inch patty. Place meat in the hot pan and cook 1 minute on each side. Taste the mini patty to help you adjust seasonings.

Divide meat loaf mixture into 4 equal parts by scoring the meat before you form patties. Form 4 equal oval patties 1-inch thick. Add 1 tablespoon extra-virgin olive oil, 1 turn of the pan, and arrange patties in the skillet. Cook 6 minutes on each side and transfer to a serving plate or individual dinner plates.

Return pan to heat and add butter. When butter melts, whisk in flour and cook 1 to 2 minutes. Whisk in stock and season gravy with poultry seasoning, salt and pepper, to taste. Simmer gravy until it reaches desired thickness, and pour over patties, reserving a little to pass at the table.

This recipe yields 4 servings.

TURKEY BARBECUE MEATLOAF

6 servings
Source: Ground Turkey Greats

1 lb. **ground turkey**

1 cup **chopped onion**

½ cup **seasoned bread crumbs**

½ cup **grated carrots**

½ cup **bottled barbecue sauce divided**

2 teaspoons **Worcestershire sauce**

1 teaspoon **minced garlic**

¾ teaspoons **pepper**

Vegetable cooking spray

In medium bowl combine turkey, onion, bread crumbs, carrots, 1/4 cup barbecue sauce, Worcestershire, garlic and pepper.

In 9-inch pie plate, sprayed with vegetable cooking spray, shape meat mixture into round loaf. Drizzle top of loaf with remaining barbecue sauce. Bake at 350°F 35 to 45 minutes or until meat thermometer reaches 160°F when inserted in center of meatloaf, juices run clear and meat is no longer pink.

TURKEY BAYOU BURGERS

4 servings
Source: Ground Turkey Greats

1 lb. **ground turkey**

2 scallions, (3" of green left, on), thinly sliced

1 red bell pepper, cored, seeded and finely chopped

1 teaspoon **minced garlic**

2 tablespoons **chopped cilantro**

¾ teaspoons **dried thyme**

½ teaspoon **ground cumin**

½ teaspoon **paprika**

red pepper flakes, to taste

salt, to taste

black pepper, to taste

4 toasted hamburger buns

¼ cup **mayonnaise**

garnish, (opt)

1 small ripe avocado,

sliced, for

(opt)

It's necessary to highly season turkey because the meat itself tastes rather mild. Yet, once ground turkey is cooked up, it's delicious. To do a taste test on the mixture, make a little patty the size of a silver dollar and pan-fry it in a nonstick skillet. This way you can adjust your seasonings to taste. A mayonnaise-type dressing and avocado make perfect toppings.

Prepare hot coals for grilling.

Place the ground turkey in a bowl and mix well with the scallions, bell pepper, garlic, cilantro and spices. Season to taste with salt and pepper. Gently form into 4 patties.

Grill patties over hot coals, 3" from heat, for about 5-6 minutes per side.

If desired, spread buns with mayonnaise-type dressing and top burgers with avocado slices. Serve immediately.

TURKEY BLACK BEAN CHILI WITH ANCHO VINAIGRETTE

6 servings
Source: Ground Turkey Greats

ancho chile salsa

4 ancho chiles, stemmed and seeded

½ cup **freshly-squeezed orange juice**

¼ cup **freshly-squeezed lime juice**

1 teaspoon **salt**

2 tablespoons **extra-virgin olive oil**

turkey black bean chili

2 cups **dried black beans**

8 cups **water**

3 whole arbol chiles

3 bay leaves

2 tablespoons **vegetable oil**

1 lb. **coarsely-ground turkey**

1 large onion, diced

1 teaspoon **salt, or to taste**

½ teaspoon **freshly-ground black pepper,**

or to taste

3 garlic cloves, minced

3 poblano chiles, stemmed, seeded, and diced

1 ½ tablespoons **chili powder**

1 ½ tablespoons **ground cumin**

½ teaspoon **cayenne pepper**

3 cups **chicken stock**

To make the salsa, toast the chiles directly over a medium gas fame or in a cast-iron skillet until soft and brown, turning frequently to avoid scorching. Chop the chiles and combine in a bowl with the orange and lime juices, salt, and olive oil. Mix well and let sit at least 30 minutes or as long as 2 hours in the refrigerator before serving. The salsa will keep up to 2 days in the refrigerator.

Place the beans in a soup pot with the water, arbol chilies and bay leaves.

Bring to a boil, reduce to a simmer and cook covered until tender but not falling apart, 1 to 1 1/2 hours. Drain thoroughly and remove chiles and bay leaves.

In a large, heavy pot heat the vegetable oil and cook the turkey, stirring often, until uniformly browned. Add the onions, salt and pepper and saute over moderate heat, stirring occasionally, until the onions are just golden and clear, about 10 minutes. Add the garlic, diced poblanos, chili powder, cumin and cayenne and stir together for 2 to 3 minutes, or until the aromas are released. Add the black beans and chicken stock and simmer, uncovered, for 30 to 40 minutes, or until the flavors have blended and chile has thickened.

Serve in warm bowls with a dollop of the ancho chile salsa on top.

TURKEY BURGER

7 servings
Source: Ground Turkey Greats

2 lbs. **ground turkey 97% lean or 93% lean**

1 bunch sliced scallions white and light green part only

½ inch fresh ginger, finely chopped

kosher salt

ground pepper

Combine all ingredients in a bowl. Form into patties and grill on a grill pan or in a Teflon skillet.

If using a skillet, deglaze with a tablespoon of soy sauce as needed- do not add oil. Serve on bolos levedos (Portugese bread) with lettuce, tomato and jalapeno aioli.

TURKEY CHIPOTLE CHILI WITH PEPPER JACK CHEESE CORN CAKE TOPPING

4 servings
Source: Ground Turkey Greats

2 tablespoons **extra-virgin olive oil**

= **(or corn oil or vegetable oil)**

2 lbs. **ground turkey breast**

1 medium onion, chopped

3 cloves **garlic, chopped**

1 tablespoon **chili powder - (rounded)**

2 chipotles in adobo, chopped

= (or 1/2 cup hot chipotle salsa may be

substituted)

Salt, to taste

1 cup **Mexican beer**

2 cups **chicken stock**

1 can **chopped stewed tomatoes - (28 oz)**

1 can **red kidney beans, drained**

1 package **Jiffy Mix corn muffin mix - (8 1/2 oz), prepared to**

directions on box for corn cakes

1 ½ cups **shredded pepper jack cheese - (8 oz)**

2 tablespoons **butter**

Heat deep skillet or wide pot over medium-high heat. Add oil and turkey. Crumble meat as it cooks, 3 minutes. Add the onions and garlic, chili powder, and chipotle. Cook another 5 minutes. Season with salt. Add beer and cook another minute, stirring to loosen any bits from the bottom of the pan. Add the stock, tomatoes, and beans and bring to a bubble. Reduce heat and simmer 10 minutes.

Heat a nonstick griddle pan over medium-high heat. Mix batter and cheese together. Rub grill with butter, nesting the butter in a paper towel to hold on to it. Ladle the batter to make 3-inch cheese and corn cakes. Cook 3 minutes on each side, until golden. Transfer them to a plate and cover with foil to keep warm.

Serve bowls of chili with cheese-corn toppers -- like a spicy, corn topped chili pot pie.

TURKEY DUMPLING CASSEROLE

4 servings
Source: Ground Turkey Greats

1 lb. **ground turkey**

⅓ cup **chopped onions**

⅔ cups **beef broth**

¼ cup **chopped green peppers**

2 tablespoons **flour**

¼ teaspoon **salt**

¼ teaspoon **rosemary**

1 tablespoon **vegetable oil**

1 8 oz can tomato sauce

½ teaspoon **salt**

½ teaspoon **sage**

10 garlic

½ cup **cornmeal**

½ teaspoon **baking powder**

1 egg

¼ cup **milk**

1 ½ teaspoons **vegetable oil**

In a large, heavy skillet cook turkey in oil (or you can use vegetable cooking spray) about 5 minutes or until lightly browned, stirring to break up the meat. Add onions, tomato sauce, beef broth, sage, salt, garlic, and peppers. Bring to a boil, and reduce heat and cover. Simmer for 15 minutes, stirring occasionally.

Meanwhile, mix the cornmeal, flour, baking powder, salt, rosemary, egg, milk and oil. Mix well and drop by tablespoons on top of the turkey mix. Cover and simmer 10 minutes or until dumplings are firm.

TURKEY MEATBALL MINESTRONE

6 servings
Source: Ground Turkey Greats

1 lb. **ground turkey**

2 cups **chopped onion divided**

1 cup **seasoned bread crumbs**

2 teaspoons **minced garlic divided**

½ teaspoon **Italian seasoning**

Vegetable cooking spray

1 cup **celery chopped**

2 teaspoons **olive oil**

2 Cans (14-1/2 ounces) no-fat chicken broth

1 Can (14 ounces) chopped tomato undrained

1 Can (8 ounces) chick peas

1 Can (8 ounces) cut green beans drained

1 teaspoon **sage leaves**

1 teaspoon **basil**

1 teaspoon **parsley**

1 cup **dry rotini pasta**

In medium bowl combine turkey, 1 cup onion, bread crumbs, 1 teaspoon minced garlic and Italian seasoning. Shape mixture into 36 meatballs. Place meatballs on baking pan (10 x 15 x 1 inch) sprayed with vegetable cooking spray. Bake at 400°F (Fahrenheit) for 20 to 25 minutes or until meatballs are brown on outside and no longer pink in center.

In 5-quart saucepan, over medium-high heat, saute remaining onion and garlic with celery in olive oil for 5 to 7 minutes, or until limp. Add chicken broth, tomatoes, chick peas, green beans, sage, basil, and parsley.

Increase heat and bring mixture to boil; add rotini. Reduce heat, cover and simmer for 15 to 20 minutes or until pasta is al dente. Add meatballs and simmer 5 to 10 minutes, or until mixture is heated throughout.

TURKEY MEATBALLS C/P

30 servings
Source: Ground Turkey Greats

10 ounces **apple jelly**

1 tablespoon **vinegar**

1 egg, beaten

¼ cup **seasoned bread crumbs, fine**

2 tablespoons **milk**

¼ teaspoon **garlic salt**

1 lb. **ground turkey, raw**

non-stick veg. spray

In 3 1/2 or 4 quart crockery cooker: stir together barbeque sauce, jelly, tapioca and vinegar. Cover; cook on high-heat setting while preparing meatballs.

For meatballs, in large bowl combine egg, bread crumbs, milk and garlic salt. Add ground turkey and mix well.

Shape into 1/2 to 3/4-inch meatballs. Spray a 12-inch non-stick skillet; add meatballs and brown on all sides over med. heat. Drain meatballs. Add meatballs to crockery cooker; stir gently.

Cover; cook on high heat setting for 1 1/2 to 2 hours. Makes 30 meatballs. NOTE: for 5 or 6-quart crockpot: Double all ingredients. Prepare as above.

Makes 60 meatballs.

TURKEY MEATLOAF

5 servings
Source: Ground Turkey Greats

1 tablespoon **oil**

1 cup **chopped onion**

1 cup **chopped celery**

½ **red or green bell pepper, finely diced**

1 teaspoon **minced garlic**

½ cup **fresh bread crumbs**

¾ cup **chili sauce**

¼ cup **milk**

1 egg

1 ½ teaspoons **Worcestershire sauce**

½ teaspoon **salt**

¼ teaspoon **cayenne pepper**

¼ teaspoon **ground cumin**

Freshly-ground black pepper, to taste

1 lb. **ground turkey breast meat**

Heat oil in large nonstick skillet over medium heat. When hot, add onion, celery, bell pepper and garlic. Cook, stirring often, until just starting to soften, about 6 minutes.

Transfer to bowl. Stir in bread crumbs, 1/4 cup chili sauce, milk, egg, Worcestershire sauce, salt, cayenne pepper, cumin and black pepper to taste. Mix well. Add turkey, using fork to work into vegetable mixture. Let rest 10 minutes.

Transfer to shallow baking dish lined with foil and shape into 8- by 5-inch oval; mixture will be moist. (Can be covered tightly and refrigerated at this point up to 1 day.)

Before baking, spread remaining chili sauce over top and sides. Bake, uncovered, at 375 degrees until internal temperature registers 185 degrees, about 45 to 50 minutes.

Serve hot or at room temperature.

This recipe yields 4 to 5 servings.

Each of 5 servings: 196 calories; 818 mg sodium; 86 mg cholesterol; 5 grams fat; 17 grams carbohydrates; 20 grams protein; 0.50 gram fiber.

TURKEY SPECIAL

1 servings
Source: Ground Turkey Greats

1 cup **chopped onion**

⅓ lb. **sliced mushrooms**

¼ lb. **ground turkey**

10 ½ cups **packed washed spinach leaves**

8 large eggs

3 tablespoons **shredded parmesan cheese**

salt and pepper

In an 11- to 12-inch nonstick frying pan over medium-high heat, combine 1 cup chopped onion, 1/3 pound sliced mushrooms, and 1/4 pound ground turkey. Stir often until mushrooms are lightly browned, about 10 minutes.

Add 1/4 pound (21/2 cups packed) washed spinach leaves; stir often until wilted, 3 to 4 minutes. Meanwhile, beat 8 large eggs to blend. Turn heat to low, pour eggs into pan, and stir until eggs are creamy, 2 minutes, or as set as you like.

Sprinkle with 2 to 3 tablespoons shredded parmesan cheese and season with salt and pepper.

Serves 4.

TURKEY TOSTADAS

6 servings
Source: Ground Turkey Greats

6 (6 in.) Flour Tortillas

½ lb. **Ground Turkey**

¼ cup **Minced Onion**

2 cl Garlic Minced

1 Jalapeno Pepper, Seeded & Minced

1 cn (8 Oz.) Tomato Sauce

1 teaspoon **Dried Oregano**

½ teaspoon **Thyme**

ds Of Hot Sauce

¼ cup + **2 t. Mozzarella Cheese (1 1/2 Oz.)**

¼ cup **+2 T. Plain Low Fat Yogurt**

Place tortillas on a baking sheet, bake at 350°F for 7 to 10 min. Or until crisp.

Set aside. Combine turkey, onion, garlic & jalapeno pepper in a large skillet coated with cooking spray; cook over medium heat until meat is no longer pink, stirring to crumble meat. Add tomato sauce, oregano, thyme & hot sauce; stir well.

Simmer 10 min. Or until thickened. Spread about 1/3 c. Turkey & tomato sauce mixture over each reserved tortilla; sprinkle each with 1 t. Mozzarella cheese. Broil 8 inches from heat until cheese melts. Top each tostada with 1 t. Lowfat yogurt.

Garnish with jalapeno pepper slices if desired.

TURKEY VEGETABLE MEAT LOAF

4 servings
Source: Ground Turkey Greats

1 ½ lbs **ground turkey**

2 ounces **fresh mushrooms, sliced**

3 ounces **grated carrots**

2 ounces **grated onion**

2 tablespoons **freshly chopped parsley**

Salt and lemon pepper

2 tablespoons **flour**

1 egg

Mix all of the ingredients well. Place in an oven-proof casserole dish and bake in the oven at 400° F (200° C) for 1 hour or until well done and lightly browned on top.

Serve with baked potatoes.

This meat loaf is a healthy combination of turkey and vegetables which is easy to make and can be frozen. Make it up ahead of time, freeze it and bake it when you need it.

TURKEY-CHIPOTLE SOFT TACOS

1 servings
Source: Ground Turkey Greats

1 lb. **ground turkey**

2 cloves **garlic, minced**

1 onion, chopped

1 tablespoon **chili powder**

2 teaspoons **ground cumin**

¼ lb. **kale or Swiss chard**

2 canned chipotle chilies, drained

1 can **tomato sauce, (15 oz.)**

8 nonfat flour tortillas, warmed

1. In a 12-inch nonstick frying pan, combine turkey, garlic, onion, chili powder, and cumin. Cook over medium-high heat, stirring often, until meat is lightly browned, 7 to 8 minutes.

2. While meat browns, chop kale and chipotles. When meat is ready, add kale, chipotles, and tomato sauce to pan and stir. Cover tightly and simmer, stirring occasionally, until kale is wilted, about 10

minutes.

3. Transfer mixture to a serving bowl; spoon into tortillas to eat.

Makes: 4 servings

○ ○ ○ ○ ○

Index

CPSIA information can be obtained
at www.ICGtesting.com
Printed in the USA
LVHW010454181218
600852LV00014B/301

9 781488 501074